AMY GRANT IN CONCERT

The first half of Amy's shows are usually devoted to her more religious numbers, including a few moving hymns. There are quiet moments. Sometimes members of the audience will kneel. Amy sits at the end of the stage, reaching out to her fans, talking a little about her life, dispensing a bit of folksy wisdom about love and life. The second half of the show is more rollicking and rolling. Kids run up the aisles screaming. Sometimes they form chains and snake through the auditorium, singing and dancing. When Amy gallops across the stage, playing air guitar, it is impossible not to respond to her energy. This is rough and tumble rock and roll, the cutting edge of contemporary music. But it is impossible to overlook Amy Grant's inspirational message—which adds another important dimension to the experience—and that is what she is all about . . .

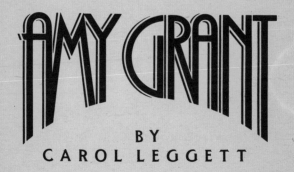

AMY GRANT

BY
CAROL LEGGETT

PUBLISHED BY POCKET BOOKS NEW YORK

Another *Original* publication of POCKET BOOKS

POCKET BOOKS, a division of Simon & Schuster, In
1230 Avenue of the Americas, New York, N.Y. 10020

ISBN: 0-671-61795-8

First Pocket Books printing August 1987

10 9 8 7 6 5 4 3 2 1

POCKET and colophon are registered trademarks
of Simon & Schuster, Inc.

Printed in the U.S.A.

To Ozzy,
wherever he is

ACKNOWLEDGMENTS

I would like to thank the following for their help in putting this book together: A & M Records, especially JoAnne Brown in New York; the many kind people at Word, Inc.; the David Brokaw Company; Warner Bros. Records; NBC; Bill Fitzpatrick at the White House; Blanton/Harrell; Melinda Scruggs at Reunion Records; Pinkie Black and Leora Kahn for expert picture help; Tony Gardner and Sydny Miner.

Also—loads of thanks to those friends who helped me keep my mind on my work and my nose to the grindstone: my dearest Blinker, Meg, Albert, Jeannette, Peter, Douglas, Patti, Marilyn, Babalu Pomerantz and K. Lee Gardner.

AMY GRANT

Contemporary Christian music. Modern gospel with a backbeat. Sometimes called Godpop—an industry "about to erupt like a volcano!" Quality rock and pop music with meaning, presented by young (like their audiences), energetic, charismatic personalities who want to spread the word about the Lord, but do it in a hip, 1980s kind of way that is accessible to their legions of fans. The music includes not only rock and roll, but heavy metal, jazz fusion, middle-of-the-road pop, soul, and country, too.

Gospel rock (gospel meaning all music that has God- and religion-directed content), got off to a slow start in the 1960s (predictably, in Southern California, at Maranatha Records); limped through the 1970s with mediocre acts, unsophisticated production values and an extremely limited network for touring and sales; and now has suddenly burst onto the scene in a big way. One of the fastest growing segments of the industry, contemporary Christian music (8 percent of all record sales in the United States, according to the Recording Industry Association) now outsells both jazz and classical music. A changing mood in this country, toward the more conservative, the more traditional, has set the stage for "gospop" to seek favor among the masses. Teens and young married couples, sick of overt sexual lyrics in mainstream rock and roll, are finding Christian music something they can dig, with a more uplifting, inspirational message—good music with better values. Parents, too, are enthusiastic about this alternative to sex and drugs in rock and roll. No more Mötley Crüe and Black Sabbath, with their threatening black leather and dark lyrics. The music is danceable and fun, and there is no need to worry about the adverse effects it will have on impressionable young minds. While Tipper Gore and her committee of mothers gain more and more public support for their crusade to ban offensive lyrics on rock records for youngsters, there is no need to do this with Christian music, where wholesomeness is a happening thing. Satan is out, and Jesus is in, and along with this original, fresh, and refreshing musical format comes a new stylishness, polished production, and a new breed of up-and-coming performers. None have distinguished themselves, sold more records, attracted more fans, or had a bigger impact on both the Christian and secular pop scenes than Amy Grant who, in 1987, is well on her way to becoming a household name.

Amy Grant, dubbed the "Queen of Gospel" by *Esquire* magazine, is an attractive, all-American girl. She has that indescribable "star quality," loads of talent, and freely admits to being very lucky. She's been called, alternately, the Michael Jackson and the Whitney Houston of gospel. She is one of four female singers who constantly fill big concert halls

Amy Grant at Harpeth Hall *(Courtesy The Nashville Banner)*

(the other three are Tina Turner, Cyndi Lauper, and Madonna). While projecting a "chaste hipster" persona, she can often be found on stage wearing a leopard-skin jacket, hot pink satin, or silver glitter boots. Her seven-piece backup band includes a crack bunch of rock guitars, electric keyboards, a hard-driving backbeat, and glossy, California-inspired pop sounds—as well as her husband (and collaborator) Gary Chapman. Amy's songs are not the usual pop fare, however. While the sound is the same, the message is quite different. The lyrics are about love ("love and belief can conquer anything— they are the only important things in life," according to Amy)—love of God, love of fellow man, love for traditional, decent, and moral values. Amy not only sings about her religious beliefs, she also deals with socially relevant issues in an upbeat, hopeful way— things that matter to her younger fans (though she is popular with *all* ages). There is music about relationships, teen temptations regarding sex, depression, loneliness, family, and other matters of the spirit. She has single-handedly smashed the stereotype of the gospel singer. Amy Grant has a completely different background from the traditional gospel performer. She has always had different goals and a unique brand of presentation, and has never counted hard-core gospel fans as her own. The only thing she shares with her "category" is her religious conviction. Grant's ascent to stardom has been a little easier than it might have been if not for other Christian rockers like Petra and DeGarmo & Key, who were trailblazers. Yet Amy's huge success has opened up a whole new set of possibilities for evangelical pop stars, who are all now part of a booming industry. Amy comments, "Gospel doesn't have to feature fat guys in powder blue suits or songs that last forty-seven minutes." So far, Amy Grant has been awarded four Grammys (the first ever in the gospel industry), can boast three gold records and one platinum, and over two million records sold. She has a deal with a major, secular music company for distribution of her albums, sold-out national tours, and her own network TV special. Her disks have been consistently at the top of the gospel charts (*Age to Age* was number one for almost three years, and was only knocked out of its spot when her next album, *Straight Ahead,* was released), and has now cracked the pop charts with her 1986 duet hit with Peter Cetera (formerly lead singer of the mega-group Chicago), "Next Time I Fall." On top of a heap of talent, Amy has great appeal, according to her manager (and brother-in-law) Dan Harrell. "Amy has an unstoppable sense of positivism and morality." She provides catchy tunes, good clean fun, filled with optimism and a subtle sense of piety. Amy Grant has done the unthinkable (and until now, impossible)—with shrewd handling and a fresh approach, she is the first gospel singer to make the crossover into the mainstream.

Amy is a Christian, something she has believed in all her life. She has often been given a too-sweet image, having been called a cheerleader for God and a goody two-shoes. Amy disputes this image. Her music is wild and rollicking—fraught with electricity. Her frankness and outspoken attitudes are just as distinctive (and in some fundamentalist cir-

The Peter Cetera/Amy Grant hit single "Next Time I Fall" rocketed to the top of the pop chart. *(Copyright © by Dick Zimmerman, courtesy Warner Bros. Records)*

cles—scandalous!) as her glitzy wardrobe, her wild mane of curly hair, and her willingness to take a chance, musically as well as spiritually. She doesn't take drugs (not even aspirin), doesn't smoke or swear, and drinks very moderately (a little wine with dinner), yet she is, according to *Performance* magazine, one of the top female performance stars in the world. There is no doubt that Amy was in the right place at the right time, and has caught the crest of a booming musical trend. She has been a big reason that the contemporary Christian music industry has turned into a huge and extremely profitable business—a 300-million-dollar-a-year industry. Two huge secular record labels are signing up Christian acts, A & M and Capitol Records. A & M (the largest privately held record company, originally started up by Herb Alpert) has recently concluded a deal with Word, Inc. (the biggest religious publisher and music company in the world—now owned by ABC/Cap Cities, with profits over $40 million a year) to distribute all of Word's nine recording labels, including Amy's Myrrh label. This arrangement has catapulted Amy into the limelight (she has expanded her audience through A & M's huge secular distribution network) and made her a superstar.

Success, as always, has its complications. Amy maintains that she's "a Christian and wants to sing about it," and that being religious should not mean that she's a nerd, or is unable to enjoy life, or has to wear unstylish clothes. Her music is simple and direct, her aim to inspire her audience without being preachy. Amy's husband and her managers have encouraged her to break the mold of traditional

Christian music, and be an original. This has produced a very modern sound, complete with an expensive stage set and lighting system. Amy insists that her goal is "to make the most incredibly hip, musically attractive package and still say something spiritual in it." While this attitude has garnered her a huge mainstream audience, fundamentalist Christians reject her mode of expression (though they seem to approve of the content). Many of them have spoken out against her—calling Amy's music "too sensual"—like Rev. Jerry Falwell, Rev. Jimmy Swaggart, and Pat Robertson. Rev. Bud Calvert, a Baptist minister from Virginia, has made rejection of Amy Grant's music a cause, and has banned it from his congregation. "She's making an appeal to the sensual, which brings on promiscuity. God doesn't like that kind of thing." Grant has no choice but to dismiss this absurdity. It is not unusual for her to receive one or two nasty notes backstage occasionally, criticizing her "evil music" (something that upsets Amy greatly) or her allegedly revealing outfits. She has been told to "repent" more than once. Amy doesn't get it. "Madonna goes on stage in her underwear and nobody says anything, but I wear necklines up to my chin and I'm in trouble." Still, Amy continues to brashly reject what people expect from a gospel singer. She sticks to her goal of "encouraging a healthy life and a healthy heart and spirit" through her music. Amy realizes that she is taking a chance, but so far, it has paid off handsomely.

There is also criticism that Amy Grant is a sellout—that she has buried her religious ideals in order to make it in the world of pop, glamour, super-stardom—a world that, because of her Christian values, people feel she should try to avoid. Amy has said over and over again that she will never compromise her religious beliefs for the sake of popularity. There is, however, no need to be churchy to be convincing. Because people often turn off at any mention of God, and since Grant's aim is to communicate with people, she is subtle in her approach. Nothing is pushed on anyone, there are no judgments. Yet, Amy sticks to her aim to "tell people how my life has been touched by Jesus" in a way that will appeal to them and give them hope. Still, she wants to approach all aspects of her life in her music. After all, "religious beliefs have nothing to do with the presentation—God is not a cultural experience," Amy answers her critics. She is not irreverent in expressing her beliefs, just joyful and exuberant. Her repertoire consists of a little bit of everything—religious anthems, driving dance songs layered with synthesizers, pounding rock, and quiet, ballad-like testaments to her guiding light, Jesus. The resounding theme throughout is staying optimistic, and Amy does not see this as any kind of a sellout—she finds it consistent. There is nothing sneaky about veiled religious references—it is better to reach people than turn them off. There is no reason why Amy Grant cannot be a presence in two worlds: the world of Christianity *and* the world of pop.

Grant got started in the contemporary Christian music field at the beginning of an era when more and more people were returning to their religious roots, led by their president, Jimmy Carter, a very vocal born-again Christian. More and more secular music personalities were publicly expressing their religious beliefs as well—Bob Dylan, Little Richard, Myron LeFevre (who has played with the Rolling Stones and Eric Clapton), Donna Summer, Leon Patillo (of Santana), Al Green, Phillip Bailey (former Earth, Wind & Fire member who had a number-one single with Phil Collins, "She's an Easy Lover"), Prince, and U2—among others. It was the perfect time for a "rock and roller with a Sunday school sensibility." Amy appeared on the scene, singing about Christian love, personal integrity and pure relationships in an inspiring as well as an exciting and entertaining way. Her vocal style has been compared to that of Karen Carpenter, Olivia Newton-John, Tanya Tucker, Bonnie Tyler, and even Janis Joplin. Amy attributes her success to her naturalness, her normalcy, her ability to talk to her fans honestly about things they have experienced in their own shared language.

Amy defies the categorizations people make about Christians, gospel singers, and feisty young entertainers from Nashville! This wholesomeness mixed with a sophisticated pop style has brought her unprecedented success. While many still try to pigeonhole Grant as a gospel singer, her distinctive fusion of rock/pop music and uplifting lyrics has carried her on a groundswell of fame. An interesting combination, it offers a wide range of possibilities—fans who appreciate her music, fans who dig her values, and a mixture of both, spanning a wide age range. There is no doubt about it: Amy Grant is one

Amy composing a song at the piano at home, 1980
(Copyright © 1980 by The Nashville Banner)

of the most happening performers in the music industry today.

―――――――

Amy Lee Grant was born in St. Joseph's Hospital in Augusta, Georgia, on November 25, 1960. She was the fourth daughter of Dr. Paine Grant and his wife Gloria. Little Amy was welcomed into the family by her three older sisters, Mimi, Kathy, and Carol. At the time of Amy's birth, Dr. Grant was doing his residency at the Army hospital in Fort Gordon, after an internship at Vanderbilt Hospital in Nashville, Tennessee, his home town. In 1961, the Grant family moved to Houston for a time, so that Dr. Grant could complete his training—then back to Nashville, where he set up a medical practice, specializing in radiology, oncology, and cancer treatment.

Amy was born into a life of privilege as well as piety. Dr. Grant's father, Otis Grant, had also been a well-known Nashville doctor, and his mother was one of the six children of famous insurance multimillionaire, entrepreneur, and philanthropist, A. M. Burton. The Grants had been comfortably upper-middle-class for several generations, well-established and respected in Nashville society by the time Amy came along.

Dr. and Mrs. Grant have always prided themselves on having a close-knit family—a family united not only by love, but also by intense and devoted religious beliefs. They have always belonged to the extremely conservative Church of Christ, attended by many upwardly-mobile Southerners. The whole family attended services quite regularly, and Gloria Grant recalls "I read the children Bible stories, practically from the day they were born," carrying on a family tradition of being heavily involved in Christianity. Gloria Grant is also remembered for sometimes overdoing it with her beliefs—proselytizing to neighbors, often being "just a bit too pushy." A. M. Burton, in his day, used a major portion of his charitable contributions for the express purpose of giving children a traditional Christian education. It is obvious that an involvement with the religious life is a large part of Amy Grant's heritage.

Amy always attended services with her parents, and even underwent an adult baptism (as is the practice of the Church of Christ) when she was eight or nine. She often felt that her mother, in particular, came on too strong to the children regarding their Christianity. It also made her extremely uncomfortable in church, to be under her parents' constant scrutiny. Besides, the music was too constrained, "not exactly a joyful noise." Amy began to feel that she couldn't express her religious beliefs freely. Later, this caused her to seek out her own church, where she could be herself, and get into her own brand of religion without any parental pressures or judgments.

The childhood of Amy Grant has been characterized as extremely normal, although she admits that she was pretty spoiled as the baby of the family. Being the youngest also made her into a bit of a rebel—always testing her family to see how far they would indulge her. Adjustment to school was difficult for Amy, and there were some problems. After years of having everyone at home make a huge fuss over everything she did, Amy didn't like being treated just the same as the other children at school. She wet her bed until the fifth grade (often trying to blame her "problem" on the dog!), but finally got it worked out. Amy had her first and last surprise birthday party in the second grade, and spent time in front of the TV like any other kid, watching her favorite show, "The Andy Griffith Show" (which her band still watches in reruns when on tour). She attended a private grammar school in Nashville called Ensworth, and later, as a teenager, went to an extremely prestigious all-girls' school, Harpeth Hall (for high school), in the suburb of Green Hills, near the exclusive community of Belle Meade, where the Grants live. Harpeth Hall has excellent academic credentials, and prides itself on the large number of its graduates who go on to college, many of them to Ivy League schools. It is described as a place for achievers, the perfect institution for an ambitious Amy.

There were the normal, adolescent-girl adjustments to make, though. Amy remembers how self-conscious she was about her appearance (something that still often troubles her as an adult), and says that her fourteenth year was the ugliest year of her life! "I had all the usual problems of a young girl— braces, glasses, acne, being overweight, having to get my mother to iron my frizzy hair." Amy even shaved off her widow's peak once because she thought it made her look like Eddie Munster. Like any other teen, Amy was confused, and disturbed because she didn't reach puberty until much later than the other girls she knew. "Everybody else's body seemed to be changing but nothing was happening to me." But Amy had her religious conviction to help her get through the trauma of adolescence. The formal aspect of her faith, the Church of Christ, was feeling more and more restricting, though, and Amy began to look for another way to express her Christian feelings.

At the age of fourteen, Amy Grant got involved, quite by accident, in a new church. She had a terrible and consuming crush on a local boy who ran an evangelical Bible Study class, and who just happened to be dating one of her older sisters. Amy set out to win this guy—at all costs. (She even announced this to her sister!) Once in the Belmont Church (where the class was held), an inner-city, non-denominational mission near Music Row, she was impressed by the zeal of the people who hung out there. Belmont, which grew out of the hippie movement of the 1960s and 1970s, had a much more lasting effect on Amy than the crush on the Bible teacher, which faded away rather quickly. In this new environment, Amy said she felt there was a "real communication with Him" going on. It all made a great deal of sense to her, even though her parents were not exactly thrilled with her new house of worship and her new religious affiliation. Amy was powerfully drawn to the Belmont, and started to hang out there. The preacl.er of the church, Don Finto, was (and is) extremely charismatic, and had real appeal to his young flock, many of them Vanderbilt students from the nearby campus. The church was always packed with kids, and Amy was proud and excited to be one of them—in blue jeans and bare feet and possessed of great energy. Amy recalls, "People would pack in. In the summer we sweated, in the winter we froze, and everyone just sang heartily." Amy was one of the first members of the congregation to introduce a musical instrument to the Belmont mass—she accompanied herself on guitar—and she began to realize that the Christian experience was not just something that existed in church on Sundays. It was for every day, and for the rest of her life.

Not only did Amy become a regular member of Belmont Church, she often visited (and at one time worked at) the coffeehouse and bookstore across the street from the church, the Koikonia—which was a big scene for the emergence of what would later be the Christian pop phenomenon. Don Finto remembers his church as it was in those days. "We had no dress codes, and we accepted anyone, no matter who or what they were—we were just trying to help people." Amy Grant is still very close to Finto, who often meets her and her band on tour to give them communion and lead private prayer meetings.

Amy's move to a new, offbeat kind of church was a big rebellion against her ultra-conservative family. In that respect, this was a very normal teenage experience. Amy tried to convince her family that her way was more right than theirs—that she had some kind of sacred knowledge they were both too thick to understand. "When you're young and discover any sort of truth, it suddenly makes you want to tell your parents how to live. They must have been trying to keep a straight face! Every parent has to go through it." The Grants accepted their daughter's newfound religious expression—and it was during this era that Amy Grant planted the seeds that would later allow her to become a big recording star in the field of Christian pop music.

As a child, Amy had always been kind of musical. She sang simple songs at the Church of Christ, played the piano at ten, and in her early teenage years got a girlfriend at camp to teach her to play the guitar—after sacrificing every one of her fingernails! Amy was always a very enthusiastic pop fan, and listened to Elton John, Carole King, James Taylor, and John Denver. When she played and sang, Amy's musical choice was always pop. She was a gifted singer, and thoroughly enjoyed the experience. At Harpeth Hall, Amy began to write a few songs. It was the first time that she "accepted the full force that God loves me." Of her first compositions, "I had songs in my repertoire for everything but my spiritual experience—the good and the struggle it brought into my life." Besides, there weren't any existing songs that appealed to Amy or reflected her personal interests and beliefs. It was at this point that Amy Grant started writing Christian songs.

Life at Harpeth Hall was a happy experience. Amy was popular with her classmates, and active in clubs, theater productions, and in student government. In her senior year, she was awarded the honor of Lady of the Hall—given to the most liked, respected, and excellent all-around student. Amy was also voted Most Talented. While she never really craved the spotlight (and still insists that this is not one of her major considerations in her performing career), and felt that her shyness held her back a bit, Amy still performed informally for the other girls, singing about her belief in God and her firm and traditional values. Because of her deep religious feelings and her ability to articulate them to her peer group, Amy's friends often sought her out for advice. (Her fans still do this today.) She became an unofficial counselor. All the kids were going through the same kinds of things—boys, sex, freedom, growing up, parents. But Amy had specific guidelines because of her deep convictions. She shared them with everyone who was interested, and her classmates loved and respected her—and begged to know how they could "get through to God" too.

This "nobility" often caused Amy to be categorized as a "stick-in-the-mud"—though she insists that she has always been a fun-loving girl, and had a completely normal teenage experience in every way. Like a typical teen, Amy loved her car, a maroon MG, and went through constant crushes on boys. Sex was confusing *and* exciting to her, and often embarrassing. She admits that she went as far as she could rationalize (sexually) but stopped short because "there is only one first time." Amy does, however, admit to more than a few transgressions as a kid—flunking the occasional test and getting drunk on honeysuckle wine (and barfing) on a school trip!

Ultimately, though, Amy Grant was moved to tell her friends about Jesus, and how He could change their lives as He had changed hers. "We've talked about sex and let's party, now let's talk about the eternal significance of the fact we're here."

Amy's classmates enjoyed her musical abilities, and always encouraged and supported her, as did her own family. One day at Harpeth Hall, Amy fell asleep during the Christian devotional—it was so boring! She asked if she could run a vespers service, and was given permission. Amy sang four of her own evangelical compositions, mixing them into her regular repertoire. Her fellow students were moved and deeply affected by what she had to say, and after that, Amy performed vespers on a regular basis. While admitting to becoming extremely nervous before going on, once she got there she felt right at home. "Ever since I was a kid, I've been interested in the idea of God dealing with human beings." This is a thought that Amy has built her entire career around—a career that began during her seventeenth year.

Brown Bannister, several years Amy's senior, was one of the Belmont Church and Koikonia regulars, and belonged to a local band, Homecoming. She had a serious crush on him, and hung around the Gold Mine Recording Studio where Bannister (known as the "guiding light" of Amy's career) worked. He took her under his wing, letting her hang out, sweeping the floors and de-magnetizing tapes, just for the privilege of being around the music business. Brown, a fledgling record producer and scout for Word Records (the biggest Christian music company at the time) had come into the business via Chris Christian—also involved with Word.

Christian had broken into music working for Pat Boone, and had also produced a huge-selling record by B. J. Thomas ("Raindrops Keep Falling on My Head") after he became a born-again Christian. Chris Christian also authored a children's book (Amy wrote the foreword).

Both Bannister and Christian were emerging as important figures in the new pop gospel sound, later to emerge as contemporary Christian music. Amy just happened to make a tape of her compositions for her parents, which, incidentally, all had some Christian implication—"vulnerability and spiritual resolve." Brown had promised to dupe the tape so that Amy would have a copy, and heard it then—liking it very much, and recognizing its unique and commercial quality. Bannister played the tape for Chris Christian, who agreed that Amy had a lot of talent, and a big career as a recording star ahead of her—if she wanted it. Christian sent the tape to Stan Moser, the senior vice-president of Word Records in Waco, Texas. At this time, Amy also attracted the attention of Mike Blanton, head of Word Records in Nashville, who would later team up with Dan Harrell to form Amy's management team. Unable to wait for the mail, Christian called Moser long distance, and played Amy's tape over the telephone. By the end of the conversation, Grant had a record contract. When they called to tell her the good news, she thought it was a practical joke!

At the age of seventeen, Amy Grant was recording her first album. It was a stressful process for her. "I was a total moron when I was seventeen. So naive. I was too embarrassed to sing with the lights

Amy Grant and husband Gary Chapman in 1982, the year of their marriage *(Courtesy The Nashville Banner)*

on." Consequently, most of her first album, *Amy Grant* (on Myrrh, Word's contemporary Christian label), was recorded in the dark. Half of the songs on that album are Amy's own compositions.

It was recorded in a small studio in the basement of Chris Christian's home in suburban Brentwood. Lots of musicians from the Belmont Church were used on this recording—Brown Bannister, Ron Elder, and Steve Chapman, who had all played together previously in local bands Homecoming and Dogwood. Other Nashville session men joined in: Shane Keister, Larry London, and Kenny Malone. The record was released by Amy's eighteenth birthday, and sold an astounding 50,000 copies—an impressive number for an unknown with no track record, little publicity, and a limited distribution. Amy's music was new: glossy pop riffs, but with a message that reflected her good Christian values, her love of Jesus, and her embrace of traditional mores. The timing was perfect, as a more conservative country was returning to a more emphatic religiosity. Amy was nervous—she was only vaguely familiar with the concept of contemporary Christian music, such as it was—and realized she was going to be a test—a groundbreaker. The tension of so much responsibility, especially to Word/Myrrh, which was taking a big chance with her, was often unnerving. At that point, Amy knew almost nothing about the gospel music scene. It had been Word's idea for her to do Christian music—they felt it was her "natural direction," as did she. Also, being a relatively new and open classification within the music industry, Christian music was wide open, and Amy appeared on the scene at a perfect moment. At the time, gospel-oriented music may not have been her first choice, but she was excited by the prospect of singing professionally, and took the chance.

Amy met Gary Chapman at a record release party after doing her album. He would later become her husband, after a long and difficult courtship, and would also pen Amy's first mega-hit single, "My Father's Eyes." Gary asked Amy for a date the night he met her, but she turned him down that night, and for lots of nights after that!

While still a young girl, Amy Grant had become, quite suddenly, a recording star. She insists that her life was ordinary in spite of the fame. "I was a normal kid. I loved to go to parties and have a blast. I just happened to be a Christian, and wanted to sing about it." Notoriety did, however, have its drawbacks. At college, Amy was often introduced as "the girl who writes and sings Christian songs"—as the boys would edge uneasily away in droves. She got a reputation as a prude and a "regular female Billy Graham." This made her feel alternately hurt and angry, and Amy tried even harder to establish herself as just one of the kids. This is also part of her appeal—talking about religion in an informal way that makes it more palatable—an approach that worked in a big way. Now, Amy Grant is a one-woman industry, and is well on her way to making the crossover to a secular audience. This is obvious since Amy blasted onto the pop charts with her Peter Cetera duet, "Next Time I Fall" from Peter's Warner Bros. album, *Solitude/Solitaire*. The video kept Amy at the top of the charts on MTV and VH-1 as well. This outing also gave Amy a chance to work with hit producer Michael Omartian, who subsequently produced Michael W. Smith's newest album, *The Big Picture*.

Amy had made an auspicious beginning with her first album. From that point on, she was committed to making music and spreading her message. Even though the next few years of her life and career were difficult, Amy kept pushing on because of her great will and persistent beliefs. After Harpeth Hall and her first album release, she was on her way to a new album and a college education.

From the sales of *Amy Grant*, it was beginning to be obvious that Amy herself was a "special case" in the world of gospel, and that she could have a big career if everything were handled properly. Already a local celebrity, the Grant family turned to Dan Harrell for some guidance. Harrell, married to Kathy Grant, was a young banker on the rise. He had worked, previously, on the Johnny Cash TV show—so while not having much knowledge of the gospel scene, he did have a certain understanding of show business. Dan Harrell is sharp and fast, and headed Amy in a "star direction," limiting her appearances, and building her career slowly—to huge and profitable proportions. This could be done because Dan's management company (and Amy's career) were subsidized by Dr. Grant—who is involved in other family businesses as well: his son-in-law Jerry (married to Mimi) runs Dr. Grant's chain of steakhouses, and nephew Wilson Burton runs the Grant-owned *Nashville Magazine*. With the solid financial support and infusion of capital, there was no worry about being in the black right away. Dan was able to make some very canny decisions about breaking Amy that paid off extremely well later.

However, Amy's education was more important to her parents than her musical career, and after the release of her first record, she went off to school in 1978. Amy attended Furman College, a Christian-oriented campus in Greenville, South Carolina, near the Blue Ridge Mountains. She was excited to further her education—it was a family tradition—and Amy's personal life has always meant more to her than any career or stardom. It seems that fame came to Amy, even though she was not really seeking it, and she still maintains that if her career disappeared overnight, she'd devote herself gladly to "being Mrs. Gary Chapman." During freshman year, Amy's family only allowed her to pursue her musical career two weekends a month, when she would go off on mini-tours, often accompanied by Gloria Grant or friends from Furman or from Nashville. Dan Brock was Grant's first booking agent, but she was soon inked by the Dharma Agency for concert dates. Amy's first major appearances were at the Lakeside Amusement Park in Colorado and at Will Rogers Auditorium in Fort Worth, Texas. In those days, she often ran short of material, and at the urging of the audience, would sometimes sing her songs twice!

The first few years, Amy's career was small and easily manageable, developing at a slow pace—yet she was getting a lot of attention throughout the country. At the time, the biggest gospel star was

Evie Tornquist, whose music was much more in the "easy-listening" category. Amy's less passive, more-progressive rock sound caused quite a commotion—even at the beginning, when there were no props, no elaborate stage sets, no recorded music to "fill in" the sound. She was cheered by her fans' enthusiastic response—especially when Amy was feeling insecure in her role as a stage personality. (Her early performances were sometimes quite awkward.) The Grant family was always close by, giving financial and moral support, and protecting her from many of the harsh realities of the outside world. Dr. Grant, seeing how important Amy's musical career had become to her, and understanding that she was good enough to take a real shot at it, made sure her album, *Amy Grant,* got the best available support. He hired an independent promo man to work the record in the marketplace and on Christian-oriented radio stations. Word, which was still very small at this point, didn't have the capability to really push the LP themselves. All of this paid off, and Amy was launched with style. She was invited to entertain at the Gospel Music Association's Dove Awards—they could see that she was going to be high-visibility, and it was good business to back her—so that she could garner attention for the small-scale gospel industry. Amy was thrilled with the hoopla and the encouragement, but never really identified with the gospel crowd as such—they were not her real fans. She attracted a whole new audience, outside of the rather foreign (to her) gospel environment. Amy never intended to limit her musical situation—she wanted a wide audience, and she wanted to attract not only Christians, but the secular market as well. It seems obvious that Amy, from the beginning, was headed for the mainstream.

At Furman, Amy made a few friends, but it was difficult to make close connections because she was spending her time in two different worlds, and was away from school much of her free time. English was chosen as a major, and Amy continued to keep up with her songwriting. Word was very excited about Amy's successes, and her name was all over the place. Earlier, Amy had met Gary Chapman, in Nashville. He had not made much of an impression on her, but Gary professes "with Amy—it was love at first sight"—even though it was years before their romance bloomed. Gary continued to pursue Amy in a low-key way, but she was distracted with her career and other boyfriends. After their first meeting, they didn't see each other for over six months, but Gary kept in touch via little cards and notes he would send to Amy at Furman. Ironically, it was Chapman who provided Amy with her first hit single, "My Father's Eyes" (also the name of her second album).

Gary Chapman was born in Waurika, Oklahoma on August 19, 1957. His father ran a rather noisy and exuberant evangelical ministry. Early in Gary's life, the family moved to Texas where as a teenager he taught himself to play guitar by listening to Chet Atkins records. His first gig was with a band called the Downings. While Gary gave college a try at a Christian school in Texas, he wasn't into it and dropped out to pursue his musical career—performing and writing. Soon, he was on his way to

Nashville, where he joined a gospel group, the Rambos.

In Nashville, Gary pounded the pavement and kept on writing songs, hoping to break into the big-time music biz. His first chance came when he met Randy Cox of Paragon Music (where Michael W. Smith, another big Christian "name" was working)—who hired him to be a staff songwriter. Cox first introduced Chapman and Mike Blanton. Cox, Blanton, Dan Harrell, and Gary all attended the Belmont Church as well, so the relationship was cemented through a shared faith. Chapman and Cox later left Paragon to go over to Meadowgreen Music, the gospel division of Tree International.

Gary heard through the grapevine that Mike Blanton and Brown Bannister were scouting new songs for an up-and-coming Christian singer, Amy Grant—and her second album. He had written a song, "My Father's Eyes," and had Randy Cox take a demo of it to Mike Blanton on Music Row. Blanton and everyone around Amy were quite excited about this new Chapman composition. In fact, Amy has admitted to being moved to tears the first time *she* heard it. The song turned out to be her first bonafide hit, and put her on the map.

Amy began recording *My Father's Eyes* (the album) during her second year at Furman. She was on an exhausting schedule, yet the recording process was quite exciting because Brown Bannister and Chris Christian had made the decision to make this disk very pop-sounding, and wanted the same kind of production quality used in big secular acts of the era. Amy got into this stylish approach, but sometimes had to tone things down when her own work started to sound like "drug music."

While Gary was still romantically interested in Amy, she still hadn't noticed him in "that" way. She invited him to Furman for a weekend to get to know him before she recorded his song (he was also scheduled to join her tour), but the experience was not at all romantic—they played handball and talked and the whole thing was very platonic, at least from Amy's point of view. Gary's own career was progressing nicely. He had signed with Pat Boone's record company, Lamb & Lion, deciding to stick with contemporary Christian music rather than move into pop or country. He felt, at the time, there were many opportunities in the burgeoning pop gospel area. Also, Christian music meshed more with his own personal beliefs. Gary not only secured his future as a songwriter with "My Father's Eyes," he also wrote "Finally," which was recorded by country star T. G. Sheppard, and became a big hit on the country charts in 1982. (Incidentally, T. G. stands for The Good—Sheppard!) "Finally" is a song that could be interpreted as a man/woman experience, or as a religious one. This intentional ambiguity has been the secret of Gary's success—being able to span both worlds—and it is a valuable lesson he has been able to pass on to Amy.

When Grant completed the recording of *My Father's Eyes* (she co-wrote eight out of thirteen songs with Brown Bannister, and they are published by Chris Christian's Bug & Bear Music), she was confident that she had a chance to reach a bigger audience with her hip style and her fresh lyrics. This was the most she could hope for, but fame came anyway, and ended up causing her more pain than comfort. She kept close to her family for continued support, and even included her sisters singing an *a capella* hymn on her second album.

Dan Harrell was working on his own plan to make Amy a superstar. He limited her dates (the Dharma Agency often had to turn offers down), eliminating the risk of overexposure. The Grants were relieved to have Dan in charge—they were far too inexperienced to handle Amy's career themselves, and felt they could trust a member of the family to do right by their daughter. Amy stayed away from the church circuit. There was no ready acceptance from the fundamentalist and traditionalist Christians, who objected to the rock and roll look and sound of her music. Harrell took Amy on a more pop-oriented route, booking her with major secular promoters. All of this was being underwritten by Dr. Grant, so Harrell did not have to push Amy, but let her seek her own audience slowly. It was easier for Blanton and Harrell to go a more commercial route, because this is what they were more familiar with themselves. Both Mike Blanton and Dan Harrell have ruled Amy's career with an iron hand and a strong will, and still do. When she became part of the A & M stable, Harrell made sure that strict rules were transmitted regarding Amy's bookings on TV, print interviews, and even hotel choices—only "the best" and the top of the line for Amy. She was pushed into the big time right from the start, and Blanton/Harrell have never strayed from their vision of where Amy should be.

In 1980, a still naive Amy found herself a star, with Gary's song being more than a little responsible for her fame. The touring was difficult, especially with school during the week, and music on the weekends. She became more and more separated from her classmates, and was always tired. A romance began to bloom between Gary and Amy, something Amy attributes to the fact that she and Gary were thrown together a large amount of time on the road. Gary, who is older and less practical than Amy (and more romantic), likes to think that it is because Amy finally got to know the real Gary—who is charismatic and quick-witted. Gary's own fortunes were expanding, and Blanton/Harrell signed him as a client, adding him to their small but growing roster of Christian artists.

While Amy's popularity was ballooning, she became more and more insecure. There was a huge pressure to keep the momentum going. She admits to a great deal of ambivalence at this period—she wasn't sure a big music career was what she wanted, and might instead opt for marriage, kids, and being a housewife like her mom. Yet Amy could not resist the adoration of her young fans (mostly 13- to 18-year-old girls), with whom she had an immediate rapport. They liked Amy's groovy music and her frank, totally honest approach to problems that they all shared as kids growing up. Amy often chats to her fans while on stage, sharing bits of her own vulnerabilities—showing her audience that she is often in the same boat that they are. She has the talent to make each and every one of them feel special to her.

This same frankness, which is rare in public personalities, also got Amy into trouble sometimes. In Kissimmee, Florida, during a concert early on in Amy's career, she felt so close to her 30,000 fans that she announced on stage that she was horny. "I'm eighteen and I know what everybody's thinking. I really want to know Jesus, and I really want to love Him, except my hormones are on ten and I see you all out there, wearing halter tops and getting chummy and praying together—and we're horny. I'm not trying to be gross. Let's be honest about what's coming down. Do you want to get to know Jesus? Fine. Let's be honest about who we are." This comment caused a furor in the Christian community, even among Amy's fans who felt that she had gone too far. Amy had (and still has) a tendency to blurt out what's on her mind. While some find it refreshing, the Christian establishment still gives her a lot of grief. She gets lots of press because of her brutal honesty, even with strangers. This happened in a 1985 *Rolling Stone* interview, where Amy talked about bathing naked on an African beach with a childhood girlfriend, and also spoke about seeing Prince simulate masturbation during one of his concerts. Amy's bluntness has been a bane or a blessing, depending on whom you ask. She knows that she often "puts her foot in it," but she still feels that it is important to speak her mind and be honest about her own life in order to reach out and help her fans.

The relationship with Gary developed in intensity during the tour, after some initial difficulty because of their diverse backgrounds. Amy had come from a privileged, sheltered household, while Gary had grown up with a wild bunch of evangelists. The first time Amy went to Gary's hometown church, she wondered if "God could hear their prayers with all this racket!" Gary became a very lovable member of the Grant family, and they helped his cause with their daughter, a ploy Amy laughingly calls "pretty sneaky." Gary also helped Amy with her performances, drawing from his own natural ability.

One person not too thrilled with the Amy/Gary romance was Dan Harrell. Gary was fired from the tour—Dan didn't want even the appearance that Amy Grant was "doing anything improper." Gary continued to write songs for Amy to record, but he was replaced in live performance by guitarist Billy Sprague. The relationship, carried on in Amy's spare time, began to fall apart.

This was a very troubled and depressing time for Amy, and she has admitted it was probably the worst period in her whole life. Things were not going at all smoothly. It was a case of too much too soon. There were the problems with Gary. Audiences sometimes voiced disappointment that Amy sounded "different" on stage than she did on her records. This made her feel that her popularity was waning, and she was more than a little nervous about living up to everyone's expectations of her, both personally and professionally. Christians were eager to stereotype her—could she be the "perfect Christian"? Did she want to be? Amy's ego problems got out of control. Sometimes she felt a little too big for her britches; other times she felt like a total failure. Amy started to gain weight (a fact she recounted during a Radio City Music Hall appearance, where she mentioned she had gained fifty pounds that semester and was on the way to the cafeteria for another fifty!). She was finding it hard to keep in touch with her religious beliefs, to remember she was "just a small girl in the face of the Lord—who gave me talent." Being a sophomore at college is difficult enough for any young person, but Amy just had too much on her plate. Her family could no longer keep "real life" at bay, and she had to deal with a dose of "doing time in the music business." She was a little annoyed at Dan Harrell. Amy and Gary were "two kids trying to figure out who we were, and there was this other person complicating things." After sophomore year at Furman, Amy decided that it was all too much, and dropped out of school, moving back to her parents' home in Nashville. She did not see Gary much for over a year.

Back in Nashville, Amy was able to spend more time at the Belmont Church. She also worked in the Koikonia bookstore, and sometimes performed in the adjacent coffeehouse. Even though Dan Harrell kept Amy and Gary apart physically, Gary continued to write songs for her. Five of the songs on Amy's third album, *Never Alone,* belonged to Chapman. Amy liked the "feelings" behind Gary's compositions, and their "catchiness" in an era when pop music was in a particularly dull period. Gary also worked as a song doctor for other Christian acts. His career was getting hot, especially after lots of recording acts (including Barbara Mandrell) made hits out of his songs. In 1981, Gary won a Dove

Award for the Best Songwriter of the Year—kudos for "My Father's Eyes," and also "I'm Your Lord," a hit by gospel singer Jamie Owens-Collins. Meadowgreen/Tree was backing him up, and Blanton/Harrell were managing him successfully.

1981 was a year of big changes for Amy Grant. She did some touring with the Billy Graham Crusade, and opened for the Bill Gaither Trio. She also registered at Vanderbilt University in Nashville, in order to continue her college education. Vanderbilt, an upper-middle-class school not that different in atmosphere from Harpeth Hall, provided Amy with a new lease on life. She joined her sister Carol's sorority, Kappa Alpha Theta, moved into a dorm on campus, and thoroughly enjoyed the old-fashioned, Southern school atmosphere. Amy met lots of people at Vanderbilt—it was not the lonely experience of Furman. There were lots of other kids involved in outside activities, so Amy fit in better, and was not so isolated.

Grant left the Dharma Agency, and was booked by Springhouse Productions, Bill Gaither's booking company, enabling Dan Harrell to get her bigger and better dates. Amy went on tour, playing with Christian rockers DeGarmo & Key, Billy Sprague, Mike Brignardello, Gerry Peter and Greg Morrow. For the first time, she played guitar on stage, and sang several duets with DeGarmo & Key, some of which made it onto her two live concert albums (*In Concert I* and *II*), and one which appeared on DeGarmo & Key's album, *This Ain't Hollywood*. This particular tour did wonders for the careers of everyone involved.

Performing is a snap for Amy! *(Copyright © by Todd Gaff/LGI)*

While Amy was at a new school, and touring much of the time, Gary Chapman's first album, *Sincerely Yours* (which included a duet between Amy and Gary called "Always"), had come out on the Lamb & Lion label. Amy Grant and Brown Bannister were working on a new album, *Age to Age*. This record contained the extremely popular song "El Shaddai" (God Almighty) by Michael Card & Jon Thompson, which is always included in Amy's live stage shows. A very worshipful song, Amy's performance of it is always charismatic. The audience quiets down—you can hear a pin drop. The fans grow contemplative. Amy's contributions to *Age to Age* are more light-hearted. They are a less formal approach to her religion—another aspect of Amy's popularity—her ability to make complicated issues seem easily accessible with a very human approach. Amy knows how to make almost everything seem like fun.

Age to Age turned out to be Amy's breakthrough album, and a gigantic critical and commercial success. It eventually went platinum (over a million copies sold)—an unheard-of phenomenon in Christian music. Amy and Gary had gotten together again and were dating seriously. In the fall of 1981, Gary proposed. Amy retold the incident on "The Tonight Show," (where Gary offered some marital advice to the much-married Johnny Carson). "It was a terrible day, everything had gone wrong. I was in a horrible mood, and was carrying a large bag of dirty laundry around with me. Gary proposed to me on the street, and I almost turned him down. He said that if I could love him on such a terrible day, then the good days would be easy, and we'd be able to make it through anything." Amy accepted Gary's proposal, and they were engaged to be married.

Amy was so busy with her career, she was forced to drop out of school for good. (She often says she wants to go back someday and get her diploma.) 1982 was the year that Grant won her first Grammy Award for *Age to Age*—Best Contemporary Gospel Performance. She was being noticed all over the nation, and her own brand of gospel rock was causing great wonderment among the public. Everyone wanted to hear more. There were still the hard-core Christians who thought she should stick to her more religious themes, but Amy pointed out to her critics that it would be unrealistic to sing about only one aspect of her life. While some pop critics insisted that Amy's music was too simplistic and middle-of-the-road, her fans continued to multiply. It was a hot time for contemporary Christian acts, and the various religious music publishers like Meadowgreen, Paragon, Benson, and Sparrow and Light, as well as Word, pushed their rosters in a big way. The time was right for a superstar, and Amy moved in, getting more and more attention from the Christian music establishment in Nashville. She expanded her base, started to get wider and better media coverage, and solidified her performances as she began to feel more secure about her talent. Amy became more comfortable with who she was, and was able to handle criticisms from the various arenas much better and more calmly. She had gained a clearer sense of self, and had realized, finally, what she was striving for. Amy felt that she was getting through to her audiences, and her desire to speak her mind obscured her natural self-consciousness. While Amy was still not yearning to be a big star, she did want to expand her audience—she would "go for it"—all the way. "I want to be the top singer in the U.S.A. with a wholesome image. I want people to say 'no, she doesn't sleep around and yes, she believes in God, but she's still an interesting and fun person.'" Amy, like most of us, wants to be liked, along with being accepted for her talented, stylized singing.

While many people in urban areas still had never heard of Amy Grant, her fans in the heartland responded dramatically to her new album—which was the fastest-selling album in Word's history. While Amy was busy preparing for a support tour of her well-received record, Gloria Grant was planning a large and stylish "society wedding" for her daughter and Gary Chapman—who was busy with his own second album, *Happenin*. (Michael Smith worked with Gary on this LP.) Gary had been welcomed happily into the Grant family, but he still held a little grudge against Dan Harrell, who had almost broken up the two lovers for good. Gary nicknamed Dan "Bulldog," which has stuck with Harrell through the years.

On Saturday, June 19, 1982, Amy Grant and Gary Chapman were married at the Vine Street Christian Church (the Belmont was too small, even though all the Grants were now attending services there) by Don Finto. Many people from the Christian music scene were in attendance at the beautiful ceremony. Amy wore an exquisite but simple wedding dress, and a gold cross. The reception was held at the stately Grant home on Lynwood Lane. Amy has spoken quite honestly about sex and temptations, and the period before her marriage was quite difficult for her. She felt torn about establishing a sexual relationship before the sanctity of marriage. "It was tough. There were a lot of guys I would have enjoyed knowing fully, man-to-woman, but I persevered so that I could give myself to Gary." And, perhaps, Amy can be a little too personal—"I wouldn't want to compare Gary's moans with some other guy's." Yet she is not judgmental about the sex question, and admits that her friends who did engage in premarital sex didn't seem to be any worse off from the experience. This equanimity is a part of Amy that makes her fans love and identify with her—knowing that she can accept them, even if they have done something wrong. It is the striving to do the right thing that makes Amy attractive and inspirational.

Amy and Gary went off to Banff, Canada for a short honeymoon. Later that summer, they would go off to Europe, combining business with pleasure. Gary had come to the marriage with some sexual experience, and there were difficulties in the early months after the excitement of the wedding had worn off. Part of the problem was that Amy was a little bit spoiled. Sexually, she had held herself away from Gary for so long that, when they were finally alone together, "it was like a four-month yawn." After that, though, things got ironed out, and both Chapmans became more comfortable with married life. Now, says Amy, "we have a great sex life!" She constantly fights the image that she is prudish, and while she wouldn't sing suggestive songs in concert, she might "sing a naughty little ditty for Gary" in the bedroom. Amy comes right out and says that the 1980s Christian woman is very sexual—and that there is nothing at all wrong with this. Girls can be wholesome *and* have sex appeal—there's nothing in the Bible against that! Amy also doesn't prescribe "total abstention" for kids. She feels that they should be aware of what is happening to and around them in the world, and should learn to "handle themselves."

After *Age to Age* was out, the newlyweds went off to Europe for five weeks, to tour Christian music festivals, where they both had a blast playing planned and spontaneous appearances. They opened some shows for Barry McGuire, too. Amy came home to real, hard-core, mind-boggling fame. People were not only recognizing her everywhere she went, they wanted autographs, too. Amy and Gary prepared to go on a major tour of the U.S.A., and they gave it all they could muster—with expensive lights, elaborate stage sets, and generally upgraded everything—in order to further lure secular pop fans who were used to exciting and fancy stage shows. Gary joined the tour, preferring to be his wife's partner rather than concentrate on his solo career. This pairing of husband and wife in business is quite common in the Christian music world, and Amy and Gary found that they worked together really well, without any apparent jealousy on Gary's part. He is always supportive, and urges Amy to do the most she can in the widest arena. Amy is also

Amy Grant and husband Gary Chapman share a quiet moment onstage. *(Copyright © by Gary Gershoff/Retna)*

unthreatened by her husband's talents. She constantly praises him publicly, and showcases his talents during her concerts, when Gary plays solo, then with the band, while Amy makes mid-show costume changes. "It's a great marriage. We have our fights like other married couples, but Gary's so sensitive and has such a great sense of humor."

The year 1983 was so busy for the Chapmans, they had hardly any time at home in their Belle Meade high-rise condominium with their white grand piano. A video was made for *Age to Age,* even though there were few places to air it—the mainstream outlets were not interested in promoting Christian acts. At the Dove Awards, *Age to Age* was heralded with wins in six categories, even though Amy lost out to Sandi Patti for Best Female Vocalist. (This may have been the more conservative gospel element letting Amy know they did not exactly approve of her style.) Later that year, Amy Grant came out with an EP, *Ageless Melody,* for which she won a Grammy. She and Gary also recorded *A Christmas Album* (still a strong seller) at the Caribou Ranch in Colorado—a disk that was certified gold. One of the singles from that album, "Tennessee Christmas," was recorded with most of the Grant family in attendance, and hit the country charts. Other versions were done by Alabama and Steve Wariner. This song was the first to catapult Amy onto the secular charts. Dan Harrell and Mike Blanton acknowledged that it was "an experiment that worked." Following this success, Amy and Gary traveled to Los Angeles to test the water for television possibilities. Amy said the whole experi-

Amy goes to Hollywood. *(Copyright © by Alan Messer)*

ence was interesting, but that she felt like "meat on a hook." As a result of that trip, Amy received an offer to sing "Flashdance" at the Golden Globe Awards, but declined, even though she certainly felt honored.

Due to Grant's huge success with *Age to Age,* she went into the studio right away for her next disk, *Straight Ahead,* which immediately went gold, and scored another Dove Award and another Grammy for her. (At that Grammy ceremony, Blanton/Harrell were exceedingly proud—three clients from their small roster garnered awards—Amy, Michael W. Smith, and Kathy Troccoli.) This album featured "Angels," a beautiful ballad Amy sang on the national awards telecast in 1985. She appeared on stage in her now signature leopard-spotted jacket (she had it hand-painted) and bare feet, causing the press to dub her the Barefoot Contessa. Pop fans were impressed with Amy's hipness, as well as her fresh approach and her sweet personality. The conservative Christian press jumped on her for being too worldly, too sexy, and too secular. They compared her to Madonna, even though the comparison is ridiculous and annoys Amy no end. She maintains that the message Madonna conveys to eleven-year-old girls is dangerous and irresponsible. Amy dismisses the entire subject—"I do not consider myself to be a Barbie doll with hormones."

Because of Amy's phenomenal success, A & M Records worked out a deal with Word, so that Amy Grant, the emerging star, could finally be widely available to the general public. This was a super-advantageous deal for Grant—and her big break into the secular market. It was a bold move that paid off well. This new arrangement allows fans to get Grant's records more easily in a larger number of secular outlets. For Amy, the prospect is exciting. "Reaching more people is everything to me as an artist." The A & M promotion staff can get Amy more top 40 airplay, get her more print exposure, and help to get her better concert and TV bookings. People cannot develop a taste for Amy Grant's music if they don't hear it—and distribution by a major record company solves that one big problem! Gil Friesen, President of A & M, did not know much about Amy until he attended one of her concerts, but then he became a big fan. He has said that he feels she has the potential to sell as many records as Carole King—and that's a lot! Friesen believes that Amy is a sure bet for a crossover artist, which has proven true already. Her material is very subtle in its underlying religious message, and the music, according to Friesen, is mostly about relationships. Because the sound is hot and the format so "now," pop and rock fans are buying Amy's records and swelling the ranks of her fans. The time for this seems to be ripe for not only Amy (although there is still the argument that Grant is a special case, and that not too many other gospel artists have her charisma or high level of visibility), but other Christian acts as well. Stan Moser of Word Records attributes this increased interest in gospel rock to the changing subject matter of most of the music. "At first, most of the songs were in praise of the Lord, now things are beginning to branch out—premarital sex, abortion, even computers. We are reaching a broader community, and the songs reflect this. The underlying message of Jesus and salvation are not lost." The music itself, too, is much more sophisticated, with synthesizers, electric guitars, and heavy drumming. All of this is not lost on the audience.

A & M's deal with Amy began on her 1985 release *Unguarded*. Even before this took place, Amy's career was changing drastically. Dan Harrell placed her with a New York booking agency, Frontier (FBI), though when their agent John Huie left to start his own agency, H-1, Amy Grant followed. In 1984, Amy got to open several concerts for the gigantic country star, Kenny Rogers. She also appeared with Charlie Daniels at his annual charity jam (she appeared again in 1985)—where Bibles were distributed to the audience. At the jam, Amy sang a gospel tune with Daniels and Little Richard, and made a new friend, too. She was photographed having her hand kissed by crazed rocker (and born-again Christian) Ted Nugent. With every passing show, Amy's self-confidence improved greatly (she has God on her side, after all!) and her stage performance got more and more savvy. She had become a true celebrity. To her detractors, who feel that it is somehow against the spirit of Christianity for Amy to be famous, she retorts "I don't necessarily enjoy being a famous person. I want to get my message across to people who it will help. I write songs to reflect my life, not get a record deal." Yet sometimes Amy admits to liking the glamour of it all, and she was recently overheard saying that "I am ready to play hardball in this [music] business." She is obviously working out her mixed feelings about her career and her life in public—as is her way.

Amy Grant and Gary Chapman went to record Amy's first album under the new A & M agreement, once again at Caribou Ranch. The record, *Unguarded,* performed beyond anybody's expectations. The hit single from the disk, "Find a Way," was Amy's first to hit the *Billboard* pop charts—a sure sign of crossover. She backed up the hit with a video, which was shot in New York, directed by Tommy Schlamme, and produced by Alan Goodman and Fred Seibert. This video received wide airplay on the VH-1 Network (MTV's "easy-listening, adult channel")—helped enormously by the A & M association. "Find a Way" made it to number eight on VH-1's list of most popular videos for 1985, and was offered, along with another Amy Grant song, "Wise Up," on the home video market in a compilation tape.

The 1985 holiday season found Amy suddenly much in demand on TV, as her popularity grew and more and more people in America recognized her talent and sincerity. She had distinguished herself, and sparked the interest of the uninitiated. Amy Grant appeared on Patti Labelle's holiday special, and sang "Everywhere I Go" with the powerful-voiced Labelle. Amy was also honored to join Natalie Cole, Pat Boone, and Tom Brokaw on the White House Christmas Special. On Christmas Day, Amy and Gary appeared on the "Today" show, performing "Love has Come" and "Tennessee Christmas." January 20, 1986, Amy appeared on the All

Star Celebration Honoring Martin Luther King Jr., and found herself standing next to such mega-stars as Stevie Wonder and Bob Dylan. There were also appearances on "Donahue," "Late Night with David Letterman" (where she sang with the hottest band around—Paul Schaffer's), "Good Morning America," and was constantly in one glossy magazine after the other. Crossover was no longer a dream—it was a reality.

A & M gave Amy and *Unguarded* the star treatment—special handling all the way. Gil Friesen had announced that he expected big things with this album, and told his people to go out and make it happen. The cover of the record featured four different, stark and stylized photos of Amy wearing her trademark leopard jacket. Previous to the *Unguarded* tour, the market was saturated with Amy merchandise—four-color programs chronicling tour life, buttons, T-shirts, and other mementos. The A & M affiliation gave Amy and her "people" more clout than they ever had before. Melinda Scruggs of Reunion Records (a Blanton/Harrell label) was brought in to coordinate the tour publicity, and a big-time outside public relations office, The Brokaw Company, was hired in Hollywood. Professional show designers worked carefully with Gary Chapman on an elaborate stage and light show. Commercial endorsements were forthcoming—Amy did ads for Sony Cassettes and Curtis-Mathes TVs. All the luxurious perks were available—Silver Eagle buses to tour in (with banners across the front with the slogans "Nobody You Know" and "Say What"), a

Patti Labelle and Amy Grant sing a duet, "Everywhere I Go," on Patti's TV special, November 1985.
(Courtesy A & M Records)

Natalie Cole, President Reagan, Tom Brokaw, Nancy Reagan, Pat Boone and Amy Grant— Christmas Special at the White House, December 1985 *(Copyright © by Bill Fitzpatrick/the White House)*

Amy Grant sings out with well-known Christian star Pat Boone. *(Copyright © by Bill Fitzpatrick/the White House)*

Amy sings with the choir—Christmas Special at the White House. *(Copyright © by Bill Fitzpatrick/the White House)*

Rocking out during the *Unguarded* tour *(Courtesy A & M Records)*

seven-piece band, and twenty tons of equipment, much of it donated by Yamaha. A crack backup band was put in place:

BASS/GUITAR: Gary Chapman
KEYBOARDS: Reed Arvin
KEYBOARDS: Phil Kristianson
DRUMS: Keith Edwards
PERCUSSION: Tim Marsh
GUITAR/BASS: Tom Hemby
GUITAR: Jerry McPherson
VOCALS: Donna McElroy
       Kim Fleming
       Renee Garcia

The *Unguarded* tour was the biggest Amy had ever been on, and was sold out in many venues all over the United States. It followed Amy Grant's fourth gold record in a row. Since contemporary Christian music has traditionally been popular in the South, Southwest and California (mostly with an upwardly-mobile, upper-middle-class, clean and well-coiffed crowd), everyone was delightfully surprised when she sold out many venues with a mix of crowds in unusual places, including sold-out shows at L.A.'s Universal Amphitheatre and Radio City Music Hall in New York—a place Amy once referred to in a publicity release (jokingly) as Sin City! She said she felt "really embraced" by her urban audiences—traditionally a hip, sophisticated, and tough-to-crack market. Until this tour, Grant "couldn't draw flies" in cities like New York. "There's so much music out there, you really have to

Amy in performance *(Courtesy A & M Records)*

'squeak to get the grease.'' Amy's biggest attraction is her refusal to be categorized—her musical arena is "real life"—and what she decides to do next will be interesting as well as entertaining. She downplays her Christian beliefs more these days, so as not to turn off any part of her potential audience. There is no doubt that she wants mainstream fans. "People assume that you're leaving something behind. I want to keep singing what I've always sung, but I see an opportunity to do both—to sing for a larger audience and to keep singing truth." No matter what Amy's critics say, the driving force in her career is to enrich people's lives. Whatever other perks come along with that are just too attractive to turn down, and have nothing to do with the dilution of her faith or conviction.

As a veteran of ten years in the music business, Amy Grant has streamlined her performances quite a bit from the old days, and changed her image as well. She is now more comfortable on stage, and has worked on her dance moves, since she is a little short on natural rhythm. Steve Camp, a fellow musician from Nashville, has worked on Amy's stage movement with her, and has encouraged her to follow the beat. Donna McElroy, one of the backup singers on the *Unguarded* tour, has helped Amy with her projection. It is a team effort. Amy has gone for more glitz in her stagewear. Just over a year ago, she was quoted as saying that she didn't want to worry about her appearance on stage, and "wanted to look like I was home painting the den"—non-threatening, neat, and clean. However, on stage these days, she wears pink satin pants, shimmery

Amy and backup singers Kim Fleming, Donna McElroy and Renee Garcia strut their stuff in concert. *(Copyright © by Gary Gershoff/Retna)*

An intense moment *(Copyright © by Gary Gershoff/Retna)*

translucent organdy, sparkly boots, and wildly-printed jackets. On a 1986 David Letterman appearance, Amy sported quite a fashionable black and white print outfit with matching leggings and black ankle boots. She does, however, still suffer over her lack of sophistication around the groovy pop and rock community she finds herself thrown into with more regularity now. At the 1986 Grammy Awards, Amy was set as a presenter with John Lennon's son, rock star Julian Lennon. Before the show, Amy called her husband from L.A. to complain about how unglamorous and "polite" her outfit was compared to everyone else's. Yet it is this self-effacing quality that makes her so lovable to her fans.

The *Unguarded* tour was the biggest and best-attended tour of Amy Grant's entire career. It included huge outdoor and indoor halls—though Amy prefers the outdoor dates because the audience can hear the lyrics more clearly. Her audiences are quite eclectic. There are, of course, the nicely dressed, squeaky-clean young girls with Amy Grant T-shirts who know the words to every one of the songs. There are the leather and lace Madonna look-alikes, the little Amy clones wearing spotted jackets, the hard-core rock and rollers, the middle-aged yuppie couples. At a sold-out 1986 show at Radio City Music Hall (which was packed to the rafters with a frenzied crowd that was reminiscent of a Rolling Stones concert!), a newly-exonerated, born-again Christian, John DeLorean, showed up with a group of attractive young people, Models for Christ—or, as they called themselves, The God Squad. An attractive black man, David, explained that John was a

The band arrives at Radio City Music Hall for a sold-out performance. *(Copyright © by Todd Kaplan/Starfile)*

huge fan of Amy's, and that everyone in the group had all of her records. The group's Tuesday night Bible Study session had been canceled so that everyone could attend the concert. David insisted that he had "been living life to the max," a real hedonist, "until God saved me." He had been put off at first by Amy Grant's glitter and glitz—he felt her message was obscured by too many glamorous trappings—then learned not to judge, and to "accept the message in any form that it comes." Nearby, there were two heavy metal maniacs wearing Stryper T-shirts and long, shaggy hair. Art Garfunkel, who has just released a Christmas album with Amy *(The Animals' Christmas)* attended, and a group of kids with their parents were taking Instamatic pictures of themselves in the lobby—"Smile and say Jesus!"

The *Unguarded* tour features a slick, hard-rocking band full of electric guitars, keyboards, and a heavy backbeat. The first half of Amy's shows are usually devoted to her more religious numbers, including a few moving hymns. Her dress is usually more subdued during this portion of the show. There are quiet moments. Sometimes members of the audience will kneel. Amy sits at the end of the stage, reaching out to her fans, talking a little about her life, dispensing a bit of folksy wisdom about love and life. The second half of the show is more rollicking and rolling. Kids run up the aisles screaming. Sometimes they form chains and snake through the auditorium, singing and dancing. The band plays some mean licks, including a 1940s tribute to Amy's Mom and Dad, "Fat Baby," complete with Law-

Amy in a pensive mood *(Courtesy A & M Records)*

Amy's fans pay tribute. *(Copyright © by Todd Kaplan/Starfile)*

The band takes their bows. *(Copyright © Todd Kaplan/ Starfile)*

rence Welk bubbles and a cascade of balloons. "I Love You," a song about Amy falling in love with Gary, is almost always included. In the second half of the show, Amy sports her more exotic stage outfits, and gets down with the rest of the band. It's rough and tumble rock and roll all the way—the cutting edge of contemporary music. Amy gallops across the stage, playing air guitar. It is impossible not to respond to her energy. While this is entertainment at its best, there is no ignoring the fact that Amy Grant is different. It is impossible to overlook her inspirational message—which adds a whole, other important dimension to the experience—and that is what she is all about.

For Amy, the tour was a very emotional experience. Life on the road was "more difficult than I ever expected." And sometimes tedious. The band once drove nonstop from Denver, Colorado to Jacksonville, Florida! But to compensate there is the sense of family, and the chance to see and reach out to an entire nation, and most of all, to expand her horizons. In keeping with her religious beliefs, there are certain rules on tour. Drugs are forbidden, and the unmarried band members on the road are not allowed to "entertain" members of the opposite sex in their rooms. Don Finto often leads the band in prayer before concert appearances. Yet Amy doesn't want to be dismissed as an uninteresting person with nothing to offer but spiritual advice. "I'm fighting stereotype. I've got a husband I want to be real sexy with. I want to feel like a woman. I want to have fun—be the kind of person other people invite to parties. I like the Christian aspect of my life, but I don't want it to be baggage from the label Christian." She also laughs when she walks into a room: all the drugs vanish, and people start using words like "heck"!

After Amy's main tour, she did several mini-tours in 1986, using different opening acts. Some of the dates had to be canceled due to throat strain, but she was soon back on the road. Grant also recorded two duets early in the year—"Friends," with gospel singer George Beverly Shea, and "Create in Me," with her mentor Brown Bannister. There is no doubt that fame had changed her life.

One of the perks that Amy says was "right up there with meeting the President" was the purchase of Riverstone Farm—a two-hundred-acre farm in Williamson County outside of Nashville near the Harpeth River (the Chapmans allegedly paid over $1 million for it). When not on tour, the Chapmans are at home on this historic site. Amy's brother-in-law Jack Verner (married to Mimi) raises cattle on the land, and he and Mimi live in a second house on the property. It is a family affair!

Amy, who yearns to be the "perfect housewife" (even though she can't exactly cook, is not good at housework, and still has terrible trouble finding things at the grocery store), wouldn't care if her career vanished. "I'd stay at home and have babies and be quite content to be Mrs. Gary Chapman." Amy and Gary already have a dog, Reggie, with whom they are often photographed, a horse, Bar Gold, and used to have a pig, Clover. Clover was a gift from John Huie one Christmas, and was a pet until it gained 450 pounds, at which point it became dinner! In Amy's few spare moments, she likes to read a good book, forces herself to go to exercise class, and spends lots of time with her family, with whom she is extremely close—she even gives her song royalties to her sisters as gifts. But, Gary says, the Grants do not spoil Amy because of her stardom—"she has to get up and do the dishes like everyone else." Christmas is always a traditional time for the Grants to get the whole family together for a progressive Christmas dinner. And Amy and Gary get involved in their charities—food drives and teen drug rehabilitation. The 1986 Christmas season was a pretty exciting one for Amy—with the release of her album with Art Garfunkel, her soar to the top of the charts with the Peter Cetera duet and their video, seen on heavy MTV rotation and on network video shows all over the country. And, as if to prove that Amy has successfully made the crossover into mainstream pop, on December 21, Amy Grant hosted her own NBC television special, "Home for the Holidays," starring Gary Chapman, Art Garfunkel, Jimmy Webb, Ed Begley Jr. (of "St. Elsewhere"), Dennis Weaver, and Kaleena Kiff. The week previous to the air date, Amy made the rounds of talk shows, including "The Tonight Show" with Johnny Carson (she and Gary sang "Tennessee Christmas") and "Today," where host Bryant Gumbel embarrassed Amy by asking her if a certain piece of information was true. The secret, announced on network TV, turned out to be correct. Amy and Gary are expecting their first child in August, 1987. Amy has often said that she put off having a baby to get her career going, and it is

Amy Grant hosts her first NBC TV special, "Headin' Home for the Holidays," Christmas 1986; *left to right:* **Dennis Weaver, Kaleena Kiff, Jimmy Webb, Amy, Ed Begley Jr. and Art Garfunkel.** *(Copyright © by National Broadcasting Co.)*

obvious that she feels it is now established enough to start a family. She is the first one to admit that she doesn't want to be a pop singer her whole life, and is looking forward to "car-pooling my kids around" and doing many other unglamorous things she yearns for.

Amy Grant's high visibility, charm, and forth-rightness have made her good copy for the press. In the last year, she has appeared in such diverse publications as *Ladies Home Journal, Rolling Stone, Elle, Glamour, Mademoiselle,* the *New York Times,* the *Washington Post, Contemporary Christian Magazine,* and the *Saturday Evening Post* (Amy was on the cover). Amy has admitted being "a bit embarrassed" by things she has said off the cuff, or things that have been twisted around by the media to make her seem more controversial. The *Rolling Stone* interview was a perfect example—Amy said she felt that because of the magazine's trendy focus, they twisted her words to fit their mold, and made it sound like she was obsessed with sex. "They didn't get the picture of the whole person."

Like it or not, Amy Grant, as she ascends to public life, is experiencing a celebrity that is some-times difficult for her (she often feels like "running away to Switzerland"). Amy is a new breed of per-former. On the one hand, she is a contemporary Christian singer, whose inspirational message is an important part of her allure. In an age of raunchy and offensive rock music, Amy is a breath of fresh air, and has an attraction that spans many age groups and mixtures of people. But she is also a pop singer. Amy is a big fan of this genre personally—

her own record collection includes Paul Young, Don Henley, Cyndi Lauper, Scritti Politti, and Kenny Loggins. She wants to take a chance and go for complete crossover, having the best of both worlds. Amy asks the question "Why isolate yourself? Your life isolates you enough." Stardom is attractive and exciting, but she doesn't want to abandon her Christian values—or even *seem* to be abandoning her religious beliefs. It is a difficult line to tread, and the fact that Amy wants to be a pop singer (and maybe even do some acting) makes some of her Christian audience suspicious. There has been a wide range of criticism, from fundamentalists banning her "Disco Jesus" sound, traditionalists who think the way she dresses and her mode of expression (rock and roll) are somehow against the true spirit of Christianity, and others who say Amy has "used" the burgeoning field of contemporary Christian music to "get her foot in the door" of pop superstardom. And, there are the disgruntled few who accuse Amy of selling out her religion entirely.

While it is true that Amy plays down her religiosity these days, and goes for a more uplifting message in a more ambiguous but universal manner, Grant insists that she is no sellout. Amy has stuck to her original aim—to make people feel that there is hope, and that God loves them. She feels it would be dangerous to base her image of herself on other people's opinions, yet seems unsure of her place in the pop world. Amy obviously wants to bridge the gap between the world of Christian music and the world of pop. She has, according to Dan Harrell, single-handedly brought "contemporary gospel music into the 1980s." Amy is sometimes embarrassed by her brother-in-law's zeal about her mainstream possibilities. She realizes that the whole contemporary Christian music issue is sensitive—with people ready to criticize on both sides. As she tries to walk the thin line, delicately, while trying to get what she wants—recognition and an expanded audience—Dan Harrell hinders her diplomacy by comparing her to Tina Turner ("He's fixated on the fact that we both wear spandex pants") and saying that if "Quincy Jones—*the* top pop songwriter—called tomorrow, we'd go for it!"

Amy doesn't want fame if it interferes in any way with her family. She has priorities—she wants fame, but not at any cost. There are intimations of a certain amount of manipulation of her career by Blanton/Harrell (who manage every aspect of Amy's business life), and it is certain that Gary Chapman's ambitions play a big role in Amy's aspirations. "There are people around me with big dreams." Yet Amy seems to have control over her own destiny, and it seems certain what it will be. Music and spreading the message are most important to Amy Grant. "Creativity brings the most exhilarating sense of freedom." And helping others brings peace to her heart—her fans really relate to all of this, and Amy responds to each and every one of them with patience, zeal, and healing ideas about the Lord. Music helps Amy with her own troubles, and she wants to help others, too. She gives this comfort and inspiration and hope in a fresh, modern musical style, making her performance serve lots of different functions—help for the heart and soul, and a good time for all. With good taste and sensitivity, Amy helps her audience to see that there is a choice, an alternative. "I've lived a full and good life. God has allowed me to be where I am, and I do believe I'm in the right place at the right time. One thing I've never prayed for is stardom."

DISCOGRAPHY

ON MYRRH/WORD

1977: *Amy Grant*
1979: *My Father's Eyes*
1980: *Never Alone*
1981: *Amy Grant in Concert—Volume I*
1982: *In Concert—Volume II*
1982: *Age to Age*
1983: *A Christmas Album*
1983: *Ageless Melody* (EP)
1984: *Straight Ahead*

A & M RECORDS (Distribution)

1985: *Unguarded*
1986: *The Collection*

COLLABORATIONS

1985: *Do Something Now* (Christian Artists to Save the Earth), Sparrow Records
1986: *The Animals' Christmas* (by Jimmy Webb), with Art Garfunkel, CBS Records
1986: "Next Time I Fall in Love" (single), with Peter Cetera, Warner Bros. Records

Amy collects her 1985 Grammy Award for *Un-guarded*. *(Copyright © UPI/Bettmann Newsphotos)*

AWARDS

GRAMMYS (National Academy of Recording Arts and Sciences)

1982: Best Contemporary Gospel Performance
       (*Age to Age*)
1983: Best Female Gospel Performance
       (*Ageless Melody*)
1984: Best Female Gospel Performance
       ("Angels," from *Straight Ahead*)
1985: Best Female Gospel Performance
       (*Unguarded*)

DOVE AWARDS (Gospel Music Association)

1983: Contemporary Gospel Album of the Year
       (*Age to Age*)
1984: Gospel Artist of the Year
1985: Contemporary Gospel Music Album of the
       Year (*Straight Ahead*)
1986: Gospel Artist of the Year

TV APPEARANCES

"Headin' Home for the Holidays"
(The Amy Grant Special)
"The Tonight Show" (with Johnny Carson)
"Late Night with David Letterman"
"Good Morning America"
"Today"
Macy's Thanksgiving Parade

Amy Grant

Tribute to Martin Luther King Jr. Special
Christmas Special from the White House
Patti Labelle Special
"Donahue"
"Entertainment Tonight"
"Nightline"
"Merv Griffin"
"Salute to Lou Rawls"
"Story Songs & Stars" (with Paul Williams)
"Hee-Haw"
"CBS Morning News"

CHRISTIAN
SUPERSTARS
AND PIONEERS

Contemporary Christian music is a big and booming business in the 1980s, and is reaching newfound heights of popularity. It now outsells jazz and classical music, and is reaching out to a large and interested audience. Because of the huge (and mainstream) success of Amy Grant, the doors are opening for other Christian pop and rock acts, who are getting major exposure—on records, in concert halls, in print, and on radio and television. As this brand of music becomes more popular, new artists are emerging daily, and some who have been around are finally beginning to really make it. The list includes the happening songstress, Sandi Patti—also Leslie Phillips, Michael W. Smith, Petra, De-Garmo & Key, Kathy Troccoli, Russ Taff, George Beverly Shea, Sandy Brock, Phillip Bailey, and the many performers who have worked directly with Amy Grant—Steve Taylor, Bob Bennett (who was on Amy's *Unguarded* tour), and Chris Eaton, a British boy who pens many of Amy's songs, and occasionally does a stint as her opening act.

Christian pop music is a happening thing, and just seems to keep on growing. Many of today's stars are inevitably headed for superstardom. Audiences respond not only to the catchy, modern, and inventive music, but to the underlying message as well—that the quality of life can be improved by spiritual beliefs. We have been shown that music can be more than a mindless entertainment, and that there is more than sex and drugs to rock and roll.

MICHAEL W. SMITH

Michael W. Smith, like Amy Grant, is a good-looking, clean-cut, new breed of Christian pop singer
who seems destined to break through into the mainstream of pop music. His sound has been described
as "fresh" and the *Los Angeles Times* dubbed him
"the Barry Manilow of the Pat Boone set." His
energetic rock and roll is accessible to the teenagers
who form his core audience—10- to 18-year-olds—
mostly girls who respond to Smith's "cuteness."

Not only is Michael Smith a talented performer,
he is also a very successful tunesmith, writing between 100–150 songs a year! He has written hits for
Pat Boone, Amy Grant, Sandi Patti, Kathy Troccoli,
and the Bill Gaither Trio—many of them going to
the top of the gospel charts. Smith was very instru-
mental in Amy Grant's Grammy-winning platinum
record, *Age to Age,* having contributed two out-
standing songs to it, "Arms of Love" and "Got to
Let it Go." *Age to Age* has the distinction of having
been the fastest-selling album in gospel history.

Michael Smith at the 1987 Dove Awards *(Copyright © by Jonathan Newton/The Nashville Banner)*

Smith calls his own style "hip praise music," and often finds himself with screaming girl groupies of the teenage variety, who like his suave style and his catchy tunes with a message. Michael makes a conscious effort to stick to the subjects he feels are important to kids. "I want to give them something they can dig, but with underlying Christian principles."

Michael W. Smith was born in Kenova, West Virginia, where he became a Christian at the age of ten. He had always planned to dedicate his life to God, but after high school, Smith went wild. Frustrated with his music, Michael found himself into a lot of partying and some pretty heavy drugs. Then, rediscovering the Lord, he was able to save himself. This experience makes him very receptive to the problems of today's teens. Michael offers them help over the rough periods of their lives—adolescence—and tells them "to be on guard against Satan every minute!"

In 1978, Smith moved to Nashville to pursue his career in music, and things happened very quickly for him. After playing the local club scene for a short time, he joined the gospel group Higher Ground, and also became a staff songwriter at Paragon Music, a religious music publisher. While there, Michael worked with Bill Gaither, Gary Chapman (Amy Grant's husband), and Bob Farrell. In 1981, he left Paragon for Meadowgreen Music, the gospel division of a major publishing company. In addition, there were writing gigs for the Christian Broadcasting Network and studio session work. During this period, Michael was married to Debbie, who became not only his wife, but his writing partner—an arrangement quite common in the world of Christian pop, where music is often a family affair. Recently, the Smiths had a son, Ryan, an experience that has brought them both "closer to the Lord."

In the early 1980s, Smith toured with Amy Grant for two years, playing keyboards and often functioning as her opening act. His first album, *The Michael Smith Project,* sold 200,000 copies, making it one of the fastest-selling Christian debut albums! That same record was nominated for a Grammy—wonderful feedback for a novice performer. Michael has been nominated for four Dove Awards in the last few years, winning one in 1985 for Best Songwriter of the Year. His second album, *Michael Smith 2,* won a Grammy, and included many songs co-written with Debbie Smith, Amy Grant, Gary Chapman, and Mike Hudson. One of the cuts, "Restless Heart," has Smith teaming up on a duet with Amy Grant. *Michael Smith 2* was backed up by a 52-city national tour, and Smith joined the extensive Kathy Troccoli *Friends Tour.* He is proud to say that his shows feature professional lighting, staging, and sound comparable to major secular pop acts. He feels this is very important in the coming era of gospel rock—which has not always been known for quality presentation on records or in concert. Michael has also done a video, *A Way,* which will help him reach an even wider audience.

Smith's sound is a lively mix of synthesizer-based music and a heavy rock and roll backbeat. A bit of reggae is often mixed in, and he has also written some truly beautiful and inspiring worship music. Michael continues to be the Renaissance man of Christian pop, now that he has moved into producing other artists while still pursuing a writing and a performing career. Having learned to play music at the age of eight (his grandmother taught him), Smith admits to being a devoted Beatles fan, and to having been influenced by Elton John, Michael McDonald, and Bach. He has been compared to Alan Parsons (of the Alan Parsons Project) and speaks of Don Henley and Billy Joel as "competition." This young man has presence, and an ego that can't be overlooked, but he is devoted to his religious beliefs as well. He insists that kids are getting sick of "trash music" and seek a kind of music that is fun to listen to, but is intrinsically "good." Michael cites the Prince-penned Sheena Easton recording, "Sugar Walls," as music that makes him sick because it goes too far. He believes that one can live in the rock world and not get corrupted. "For one thing, kids like to rock and have a good time. They see this young, reasonably good-looking guy up on stage having fun, just like them. And, at the same time, it's obvious that he really loves the Lord." This, in his view, is the secret to Michael Smith's success, along with the fact that he communicates with his audience on their own wavelength.

In the spring of 1986, Michael Smith began recording his third album, *The Big Picture,* in London and New York, with Joe Poloker, a man who has engineered albums by Phil Collins and the Thompson Twins. He has also signed with Amy Grant's management team, Blanton/Harrell, and is involved in the same Word/A & M distribution deal that has helped Amy Grant's career so much. Smith has garnered an even larger audience, and his future looks more than promising. He attributes his vast accomplishments to the Lord, and to Mike Blanton and Dan Harrell. He thanks, also, the community of Christian performers, who are like a huge, supportive family.

Smith's life also includes extensive charity work. He is particularly devoted to helping feed the poor. Taking a cue from Kenny Rogers, Michael asks his fans to bring canned goods to his concerts, so they can be distributed to the hungry people who need them. Amy Grant is also involved in this effort.

Michael Smith continues to be a multi-faceted and talented figure on the Christian pop music scene, and his legion of fans grows daily. He is a man of few words, who lets his mainstream sound do the talking—and his message of God and good Christian values is heard loud and clear.

DISCOGRAPHY

1982: *The Michael Smith Project*
1984: *Michael Smith 2*
1986: *The Big Picture*

SANDI PATTI

Sandi Patti, a three-time Grammy winner, also has thirteen of the Gospel Music Association's Dove Awards to her credit. She is a contemporary Christian singer who plays to sellout crowds all over the world, and she is also a thirty-year-old housewife who once only wanted to teach high school music class. The daughter of a music minister, Sandi was born in 1956 in Oklahoma City, becoming a Christian at the age of eight. As a young girl, she played piano and toured with the family singing group, the Ron Patti Family. The Pattis moved from Oklahoma to Phoenix, Arizona, and then to San Diego. Sandi went to Indiana to attend Anderson College as a music major; there she met and married her husband and manager, John Helvering, who encouraged her to become a gospel performer. For their first foray into the music business, Sandi and John recorded and pressed their own record, *For My Friends*. There were also a few performances around campus.

Unlike Amy Grant, Sandi Patti spent most of her early career performing at special Christian festivals and concerts, on the road much of the time. She also did commercial jingle work before her gospel career took off—a career she and her husband call "a gift from the Lord." Patti's singing took the contemporary Christian community by storm, and she caught on just as quickly with the fans. In 1979, she became an artist on the Benson Company's Impact label, and released her first major album, *Sandi's Song,* that same year. Afterward, John Helvering took over all of the business aspects of the singer's career (he was a business major in college), and "one thing just led to another." The Helverings put together a small tour in 1980, and Sandi got a big break when Bill Gaither asked her to come along on his own band's national tour to sing backup. Later on, Miss Patti toured with the Imperials, and also with Larnelle Harris.

After the success of *Sandi's Song,* Patti went on to record five more albums for Benson/Impact: *Love Overflowing* (1981), *Sandi Patti Live* and *More Than Wonderful* (both 1982), *The Gift Goes On* (1983), and *Songs from the Heart* (1984). *Hymns Just for You* (1985) was pressed by the Helvering Company. In 1986, Patti made a new record deal with prestigious Word Records, with the built-in advantage of a distribution deal with A & M Records, allowing her, too, to be available in a wider market than ever before. Her most recent album, *Morning Like This,* went to the top of the gospel charts, produced Patti's first gold album, and won her a third Grammy.

Sandi Patti is an extremely devout Christian with a "God-gifted voice that can lift, inspire, and heal." Her most important goal (with her singing career) is to communicate and share her faith with her audience. Unlike many of the other Christian stars, Sandi does not address socially relevant themes so much as religious ones, and professes no interest in breaking into the secular market—also another pointed distinction from most of her peers. Her music, which is presented in a contemporary, pop-inspired way, can never, according to her, be as affecting as her ultimate message—which is close in content to traditional gospel music. But Patti insists that in spreading the message of the Lord, "there should be something for everyone." Sandi is happy with the new quality production seeping into the Christian music industry, and is proud to be a part of it. She sadly notes, however (when asked about "sellouts"), that some of the Christian contemporary community may just be in it for the money, and find gospel rock an easier category to break into than straight pop—but she adds that the majority are true believers like herself. Mrs. Helvering also prides herself on being as good a housewife as she is a singer. The Lord and her family have always been important to her, though her career "still means a lot to me." John and Sandi recently welcomed a new addition to their household, a baby daughter, Anna. Sandi explains that having a child has affected her life intensely. "After Anna was born, it caused me to take everything I do much more seriously."

This has been a busy time in Sandi Patti's career. At the end of 1985, she sang two songs by

"Sesame Street" Emmy-winner Joe Raposo on an animated ABC movie, *The Kingdom Chums,* which portrays the story of David and Goliath. During the huge Liberty Celebration in New York on July 4, 1986, Sandi's version of "The Star-Spangled Banner" was used in the finale of the ABC telecast. This honor (which was a complete surprise to the Helvering household!) brought an invitation to visit Vice President Bush in Washington, D.C.—but Sandi had already accepted an invitation (her first) to appear on "The Tonight Show" on the same day. Johnny Carson liked her so much, she was invited back on the Carson show in December 1986. Patti also appeared in the NBC "Christmas from Washington" special, and "A Worldwide Christmas Celebration," simulcast from around the world, starring Prince Charles, Billy Graham (Patti has sung on his crusade), Placido Domingo, Cliff Richard, and the Vienna Boys Choir—exalted company for an "unknown"! Sandi continues to get more and more media attention, and has recently appeared on ABC's "World News Tonight," "Entertainment Tonight," "PM Magazine" and CBS's "Nightwatch."

1986 also marked a big milestone for the singer—Sandi turned a joyous thirty years old! She threw a party for her friends and family, and gave *them* all gifts—to let them know how much they meant to her. She also established the Friendship Club, through which she corresponds with kids all over the world. Sandi Patti is happy that she has been able to reach so many with the Lord's message, and looks forward to continuing on her musical path of enlightenment.

DISCOGRAPHY

1979: *Sandi's Song*
1981: *Love Overflowing*
1982: *Sandi Patti Live*
       More Than Wonderful
1983: *The Gift Goes On*
1984: *Songs from the Heart*
1985: *Hymns Just for You*
1986: *Morning Just Like This*

PETRA

Bob Hartman, Mark Kelly, John Lawry,
John Schlitt, Louie Weaver

Petra is a hard-rocking band, yet their message is
distinctly evangelical. The band was formed in 1972,
when four young guys met at the Christian Training
Academy in Fort Wayne, Indiana. Bob Hartman,
devoted to his religion as well as his music, formed a
band with three friends—John DeGroff, Bill Glover,
and Greg Hough. Their aim was to spread the gospel, but in a more exciting and contemporary way
than was usually the case with Christian singers of
that era. It was difficult at first—many traditionalists
were horrified to hear the Lord's message spelled
out with driving guitars and wild drumming, but
Petra persisted.

The band played around the Fort Wayne area
until 1973, when they traveled to Nashville to audi-
tion for Word's newly-formed Myrrh label. They
were signed immediately, and recorded their debut

Petra *(Copyright © by Alan Messer, courtesy Firstborne Productions)*

album, *Petra,* in Illinois at a small studio. That first LP was not much of a success; the band and its producer were still a bit too new at the recording game. There was also heavy resistance among Christian book and record stores—they were leery of stocking a rock album, no matter what the lyrical content was. Myrrh backed Petra for a second album, *Come and Join Us*—with a new, guest vocalist, Greg X. Volz, who joined the group permanently in 1981.

The sound of Petra's second disk was even more driving than the first, since it was modeled after secular contemporaries like Styx, Rush, and REO Speedwagon. This heavy duty sound scared off Christian retail outlets completely, and Myrrh hadn't solidified their marketing strategies for this new category of Christian music—contemporary gospel pop and rock. Petra was dropped by Myrrh, but two other Word executives, Darrell Harris and Wayne Donowho, felt Petra needed some special guidance and vision, so they formed Star Song Records (also on Word), signed Petra and found them a new producer, George Atwell. This new combination recorded a third Petra album, *Washes Whiter Than,* in Florida. The band's successes were improving (if still not major), and they had a hit single, "Why Father Bother?" on the gospel charts.

For their fourth album, Petra teamed with producer Jonathan David Brown for *Never Say Die,* and pulled out a number one Christian hit, "The Coloring Song." They had finally expanded their audience with a newer, more mellow but still pop-inspired sound. In the late 1970s, Petra moved permanently to Nashville. Hartman and Volz dropped the other band members, and played with pick-up musicians until 1980, when Mark Kelly and John Slick (friends from Bible Study class) were added on, as well as a new drummer, Louie Weaver. Finally, in 1984, a new line-up was completed when John Lawry, a hot keyboardist already well-known in Christian music circles, joined the band after a four-year stint with the Joe English band.

Though Petra was experiencing better and better album sales, they were still having a hard time breaking into the gospel rock concert circuit. They finally got the boost they needed when the popular Christian rock band, Servant, asked the boys to open for their national tour. From then on, Petra launched several big, nationwide tours of their own. Their fifth album, *More Power to Ya,* was an instant smash success.

1986 brought a major change for Petra. John Schlitt, formerly of the secular rock band Head East, joined the group as lead singer, after the unexplained (and possibly unfriendly) departure of Greg Volz. A week after Schlitt joined up, Petra went off on a tour of Australia (where they are extremely popular) and Norway. For Schlitt, it was "a trial by fire!"

Petra's newest album, released in August 1986 (after the release of the double live set, *Captured in Time and Space*) is *Back to the Street,* recorded in Los Angeles, and backed up by a major, international tour—many of the dates "standing room only." Like Amy Grant, Petra also found a home with a major secular label, A & M Records. Now, they are getting lots of press recognition. In 1985, the boys were named the number two Live Band of the Year by *Contemporary Christian* magazine (number one was Amy Grant's, of course!), and they received Grammy Award nominations in 1984 and 1985 for Best Contemporary Gospel Group. While Petra's message is definitely Christian, they also reach out for the secular audience, who if they can't be inspired by the message will at least be able to groove out to the rock and roll.

DISCOGRAPHY

1974: *Petra*
1976: *Come and Join Us*
1978: *Washes Whiter Than*
1979: *Never Say Die*
1983: *More Power to Ya*
1985: *Captured in Time and Space* (Live Album)
1986: *Back to the Street*

LESLIE PHILLIPS

Twenty-four-year-old Leslie Phillips is a pretty, perky blonde with a scratchy, rough-edged voice, who dances wildly onstage and sings her heart out about contemporary themes. She has had a relatively short career—only three albums so far—but the impact of her performances have been explosive! *Billboard* magazine calls Leslie "a talent to be reckoned with." She has been nominated for a Grammy Award for her current album, *Black and White in a Grey World,* and has already made the crossover to mainstream top 40.

Phillips's music is very much in the rock and pop tradition, and she addresses her young audience, tuning into their concerns, like teen depression and suicide, sex, loneliness, and all sorts of moral dilemmas that adolescents inevitably struggle with. Untraditionally for Christian performers, Leslie Phillips appears in provocative outfits (she has even been known to flash a bit of navel à la Madonna!), has a hard-rocking sound, and has been compared to Sheila E, Pat Benatar, and Amy Grant. Because the issues addressed in her music are universal, she has become a big hit in the secular music market as well. Phillips tries to be realistic and nonjudgmental in order to speak her mind and reach out to her audience.

Born and raised in Los Angeles, Leslie began to write her own Christian music at the age of fourteen after attending a contemporary Christian music concert. She felt, however, that Christian singers were not reaching out to their widest audience, so she went for it herself. Phillips had a big break when one of her compositions, "Bring Me Through," made it onto the compilation album, *Back to the Rock.* Her popularity grew as she performed in local clubs and coffeehouses, and soon Word/Myrrh had signed her to a record deal. She now tours six months of the year to capacity crowds all over the country. Leslie has recently appeared on "Today" and on the BBC show "Rock Gospel."

This electrifying Christian pop singer really believes in what she's doing, and in her own charismatic way of doing it. "People are tired of Christian songs that are only praise and worship. The church forced the 'old' taste in music on kids. We're breaking the stereotype."

DISCOGRAPHY

1983: *Beyond Saturday Night*
1984: *Dancing with Danger*
1986: *Black and White in a Grey World*

DeGARMO & KEY

Ed DeGarmo, Dana Key,
Tommy Cathey, Greg Motton

Ed DeGarmo and Dana Key, both natives of Memphis, Tennessee, are known as pioneers on the Christian rock scene. While Ed is easygoing and Dana moody, the two old schoolmates are like Siamese twins, often finishing each other's sentences and read each other's minds! After fifteen years of struggle, this band is finally beginning to come into their own—both as performers and songwriters, having penned many hits for other Christian stars, including Amy Grant. They have also been nominated for Grammy Awards twice, in 1980 and 1986, for the Best Gospel Album, and have been honored many times for Best Album of the Year by *Contemporary Christian* magazine, as well as receiving a Dove Award nomination in 1986 for their hit album, *Commander Sozo and the Charge of the Light Brigade*.

DeGarmo & Key *(Courtesy The Brokaw Company)*

DeGarmo & Key, as a band, are eccentric and deeply religious, and they have often been noted as being bitter about their fight for acceptance in the Christian and secular music world. Unlike Amy Grant, DeGarmo & Key do not want to cross over into mainstream pop music—they insist that it isn't worth taking the chance that their religious message might be lost. While the band has been offered recording deals by three major secular labels, they continue to stay with Benson Records because of the company's commitment to Christian ideals.

Ed DeGarmo first became a Christian in 1972, after attending a concert by Christian singing star Dallas Holm. Ed told Dana about his experience, and Dana also pledged his life to Christ—in a janitor's closet at the boys' school! At that time, DeGarmo & Key were both in a band, *Globe*. After they informed their bandmates of their newfound religious convictions, they were unceremoniously booted out of the group. They formed their own band in the early 1970s, and sang about their faith, even though "there were no labels for what we did. We were just called the 'Christian band.'"

DeGarmo & Key experienced the same stubborn resistance from the religious music establishment as did the other contemporary artists who chose rock and roll as their medium. While their music was well-received, it was not by any means an overnight success. The long years on the road without too much positive feedback almost caused the end of their musical career, but DeGarmo & Key persisted, and almost fifteen years later they are finally making it to the peak of their industry. The band has definitely hit a more mainstream audience, and both founding members feel that they speak the language of the younger generation, who seem to want their inspirational message presented in a way that is not only meaningful, but fun! Also, lots of Christian teens bring their unsaved friends to concerts—and this new influx of kids translates to more and more fans.

Ed and Dana have the distinction of having produced the first Christian concept video to hit MTV airwaves. In 1985, after the release of their sixth album, *Communication,* they made a video for the LP's single, "Six, Six, Six"—which was, surprisingly, banned by MTV because of its overt violence. The short concept film is about the Antichrist (who is depicted as a suave, Hollywood kind of guy), and features a dream/nightmare sequence, where the main character becomes a human torch. DeGarmo & Key were taken aback, feeling that the usual MTV fare was and is much more violent than their own product. At this particular time, though, MTV was under especially heavy pressure to censor what might be considered gratuitous violence; Tipper Gore and her group of angry mothers in Washington, D.C., were lobbying for records to be rated so that young children would not be exposed to anything with sex or violence. (A proposal that could seriously damage and inhibit the recording industry, and might very well be considered unconstitutional.) Ultimately, the offending scene was removed and replaced by a vision of nuclear holocaust. MTV accepted this version of the video, and put it on light rotation. The incident, however, did not go unnoticed; it was covered in the *Wall Street Journal, Billboard,* and *Cashbox,* and was discussed on TV—"Today," "CBS Evening News," "Entertainment Tonight," and "Nightline."

"Contemporary Christian music has really come together in the last few years, due, mostly, to big and popular acts like Amy Grant," says Ed DeGarmo. His own band continues to grab bigger and bigger audiences, reflected on their tours (they covered 90 cities on their 1985 *Commander Sozo* tour). "There's more quality and better retail outlets and more Christian radio stations now, too." However, DeGarmo & Key measure their success by "how many people's lives are renewed by our message."

DISCOGRAPHY

1977: *This Time Through*
1978: *Straight On*
1980: *This Ain't Hollywood*
1982: *No Turning Back* (Live)
1983: *Mission of Mercy*
1984: *Communication*
1985: *Commander Sozo and the Charge of the Light Brigade*
1986: *Street Light*

ARTISTS WHO HAVE RECORDED
DeGARMO & KEY COMPOSITIONS

Amy Grant: "Nobody Loves Me Like You"
Sandi Patti: "In His Love"
Whiteheart: "Jerusalem"
Jessy Dixon: "Silent Partner," "Radiate,"
   "Spiritual Solution," "Face to Face"
Steve Camp: "You Comfort Me"
Bill Gaither Band: "Blessed Messiah"

RUSS TAFF

Billboard magazine has described Russ Taff's voice as "the most powerful, most distinctive instrument in Christian music." He has also distinguished himself by winning a Grammy Award and a Dove Award for Best Male Vocalist. A former member of the Imperials, a popular gospel rock band, Taff is now a solo artist, and often opens for other Christian acts like Amy Grant, whom Taff joined on her *Unguarded* tour in 1986.

Russ Taff is the son of a traveling pentecostal preacher. He sang, as a child, with the family band, and later, with a more contemporary group in Arkansas, the Sound of Joy. The guitarist from that group, James Hollihan, still plays in Taff's solo band. After Sound of Joy, he sang in the congregation of evangelist Jerry Savelle in Fort Worth, Texas, and married his wife Tori, who is now his writing partner. Russ has also worked as a booker for Christian pop acts in Hot Springs, Arkansas, including the

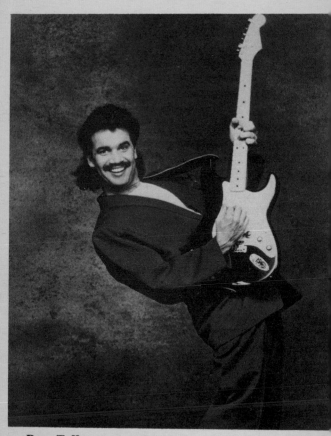

Russ Taff *(Courtesy Word, Inc.)*

Imperials, whom he later joined and stayed with for four albums.

When Russ became an Imperial, he gained recognition quickly. Their first album was *Sail On,* which was followed quickly by their second album, *Heed the Calls*—on which Taff became the group's lead singer. His signature song is from that album, written by Amy Grant's mentor, Brown Bannister: "Praise the Lord." The third Imperials album, *One More Song for You,* was a big Christian hit and sold over two hundred thousand copies, as well as producing the hit singles "Higher Power," "Eagle Song," and "I'm Forgiven." Their fourth album, *Priority,* was an even bigger hit (it was produced by Michael Omartian, who produces many secular pop acts and produced the Peter Cetera/Amy Grant duet, "Next Time I Fall"). Still, Taff decided to split from the Imperials, and go out on his own—so he hit the tour trail.

Taff signed with Myrrh/Word (with the attendant A & M distribution), and spent two years recording his solo debut album, *Wall of Glass,* in Los Angeles. It was worth the work—it stayed on the gospel charts for over two years! Russ has toured extensively, and has recorded duets with Leslie Phillips, Joyce Landorf, and Lulu Roman. His most recent album, *Medals,* was co-produced by Jack Joseph Puig, who has engineered records by Diana Ross, Kenny Loggins, and Amy Grant.

While Russ Taff enjoys his success, his R&B–flavored music (he has been called the Christian Hall & Oates) does not waver from its purpose—to spread the word of Jesus. Taff is a militant voice, with a powerful attitude and strong convictions about his spiritual mission in life. He uses music to express his deep-seated beliefs because "music is the language of the young and you have to speak their language to get through." Taff rejects the fundamentalist attitude that rock music and belief in the Lord are not compatible. This is certainly a theme that is articulated over and over again by today's Christian music performers. Like Amy Grant, Russ and Tori Taff are moving away from simplistic, overt Christian lyrics. The message is subtle without being compromised.

DISCOGRAPHY

1984: *Wall of Glass*
1986: *Medals*

WHO (ELSE) IS WHO
IN CONTEMPORARY
CHRISTIAN MUSIC

Stryper: heavy metal band; toured with Mötley Crüe on their *Heaven and Hell* tour.

Charlie Peacock: compared musically to the Thompson Twins.

The English Band: Joe English, former member of Paul McCartney's band, Wings.

Rez: more heavy metal (Rez stands for Resurrection).

Seventy Sevens: popular on college campuses; has opened for several secular groups.

Undercover: hard-core rock and roll.

A.D.: includes former members of the secular band Kansas.

T-Bone Burnett: has one foot in the secular world, one in the Christian music biz; used to be in The Outlaws; produces many acts, secular and Christian.